The Complete Cheesecake Cookbook

The Ultimate Guide Of Cheesecake Recipes

Written By :

Ellie Collins

Table of Content

1. The Flower Cheesecake
2. Bluecheese Cake
3. Lemon Cheesecake
4. Strawberry Cheesecake
5. Raspberry Cheesecake
6. Pineapple Cheesecake
7. Avocado and Lemon Cheesecake
8. Knaeh Cheesecake
9. Pistachio Cheesecake
10. Dukan Cheesecake
11. Redberry Cheesecake
12. Tuna Cheesecake
13. Smoked Salmon Cheesecake
14. Peach Cheesecake
15. Cheesecake with salted butter caramel sauce
16. Chocolate Cheesecake
17. White Chocolate Cheesecake
18. Lime and Kiwi Cheesecake
19. Coffee Cheesecake
20. Vanilla and Cacao Cheesecake
21. Lime Cheesecake
22. Caramel and Speculoos Cheesecake
23. Cheesecake with ricotta and fresh lemon cheese
24. White Cheese and Speculoos Cheesecake
25. Mango Cheesecake
26. BlueBerry Cheesecake
27. Paleo Coco Cheesecake

28. Apple Cheesecake
29. Orange Cheesecake
30. Cacao Cheesecake
31. Apricot Cheesecake
32. Tomato Cheesecake
33. Mango and Speculoos Cheesecake

1. The Flower Cheesecake

INGREDIENTS

SPECULOS Shortbread:
- 125g butter
- 215g of T45 flour
- 1 egg
- 75g icing sugar
- 1 pinch of salt
- About 25g mixed speculos

Raspberry fig compote:
- 150g raspberries
- 70g ripe figs
- 30g of sugar
- 5g of pectin
- 100g fresh raspberries (add to the cooled compote)

CHEESE CREAM:
- 450g cream cheese (Philadelphia)
- 300g white chocolate
- 150g whipping cream

WHIPPED CREAM:
- 200g cream
- 50g of mascarpone
- 20g of sugar

DECORATION:
- 3 ripe figs (purple skin)
- 100g of raspberries (about twenty)
- Edible pink and / or white and / or purple flowers

- Whipped cream

PREPARATION

1.

Speculos shortbread dough: mix the dry ingredients. Add the diced butter and crumble with your fingertips. Sand the dough and add the egg to clump and form a ball. Film the ball and keep it in the fridge while you prepare the compote. Collect the ball of dough, roll it out and place it in a square mold. Then place the dark shortbread dough in the freezer / freezer for 5 to 10 minutes and bake at 170 degrees for 25 minutes.

2.

Raspberry fig compote: cut the figs into small pieces and place them in a saucepan with the raspberries. Cover and cook over low heat. When the preparation has a temperature above 50 degrees, add the sugar with the pectin. Mix the preparation in a hand blender and keep in the fridge.

3.

Cream cheese: melt the white chocolate and let it cool. Make a mascarpone whipped cream with the cream cheese and the whipping cream. Mix the cream cheese with the melted white chocolate, and incorporate the cream into the mixture.

4.

Whipped cream: put everything in the robot's bowl and mix at maximum speed. And poach in the center of the cake.

5.

Decoration: wash the fruit and cut the figs into quarters.

6.

Assembling the cake: unmold the shortbread dough. Place a thin layer of cream cheese on the surface of the square, and a thick layer in contact with the edges of the square. Place the fig-raspberry compote on the cream cheese in the center. Complete with a thin layer of cream cheese, leveling the surface of the square with the edges. Pipe roses with cream cheese using a 1M Wilton tip in the center of the square. Arrange the raspberries, figs and edible flowers all around the poaching.

2. Bluecheese Cake

INGREDIENTS

CREAMY WITH GORGONZOLA:
- 85 g of gorgonzola
- 200 g cream
- 3 eggs (yolks)
- 35g sugar
- 2 gelatin sheets

SPECULOUS COOKIES:
- 250 g of flour t 55
- 125 g butter
- 2 eggs
- 150 g brown sugar
- 4 g of baking powder
- pm fleur de sel
- 3 g cinnamon powder
- 3 g of 4 spices
- 2 g powdered ginger
- 1 g of white pepper

LEMON CHANTILLY CREAMCHEESE:
- 300 g of creamcheese (philadelphia)
- 200 g of liquid cream
- 2 lemon zest and juice
- 1 gelatin sheet
- 35 g of powdered sugar

BLUEBERRY COULIS:
- 300 g blueberries
- 35 ml of water
- 25g sugar
- 3 tbsp of lemon juice

PREPARATION

1.

Gorgonzola cream: rehydrate the gelatin. Heat the cream and the gorgonzola. Beat egg yolks and sugar, blanch. Add the cream and the hot gorgonzola to the egg / sugar mixture while whisking. Return to the heat and cook for 3 minutes on a tablecloth. Off the heat, add the squeezed gelatin and mix with a hand mixer. Pour into the insert molds and freeze.

2.

Speculos biscuits: sift the flour and the yeast and put in the food processor bowl with the foil. Add the cold butter in small pieces and sand the mixture. Stop the robot and add all the other ingredients. Rotate for a few moments to amalgamate. Mill the dough with the apple of your hand to obtain a homogeneous mixture. Roll out 4 to 5 mm. Place on a baking sheet with baking paper. Place in a preheated oven T 170 ° for 10 to 15 minutes until lightly colored. Cut out with a punch.

3.

Lemon whipped creamcheese: rehydrate the gelatin. Grate the zest of one and a half lemon and add the juice of ½ lemon. Add the Creamcheese and whisk lightly. Add the very cold liquid cream and the sugar and beat as for whipped cream. Add the lightly melted gelatin with a little water. Mix well with an electric whisk. Place in a piping bag and refrigerate.

4.

Blueberry coulis: put all the ingredients in a saucepan and cook over medium heat. When the blueberries are cooked, mix and filter them. Keep cold.

5.

Assembling the cake: cut the blueberries in 2. Poach 2/3 of the cream cheese with whipped cream in the bottom of the molds. Arrange the blueberries and put the gorgonzola cream to freeze. Add the blueberries and finish the cream. Add the disc of speculos and put in the freezer. Out of the freezer, spray the velvet spray on the cakes. Crumble some speculos on top of the cake. Add a few blueberries. Present the Blue cheese with a jar of blueberry coulis.

3. Lemon Cheesecake

INGREDIENTS

- 300 g of cottage cheese with 0% fat
- 2 eggs
- 30 g of brown sugar
- 1 sachet of vanilla sugar
- 2 tbsp. cornstarch
- 1 lemon

PREPARATION

1.

Preheat the oven th.7 (210 ° C). Wash and then grate a lemon to collect the zest. Cut it in half and extract the juice using a fork or a juicer. Book.

2.

Break the eggs and separate the egg whites from the yolks. In a bowl, beat together the egg yolks, brown sugar and vanilla sugar. Add the whisked cottage cheese and 2 tablespoons of cornstarch. Mix everything well. Then beat the egg whites very firm and incorporate them delicately into the preparation, with a maryse or a spatula. Then add the lemon zest and the lemon juice then gently mix the cheesecake mixture.

4. Strawberry Cheesecake

INGREDIENTS

THE STRAWBERRY CHEESECAKE :
- 4 whole eggs
- 80 g unsalted butter
- 200 g caster sugar
- 500 g of cream cheese (Philadelphia type)
- 100 g of biscuits "Small-butter"
- 250 g of strawberries (fresh)

THE STRAWBERRY COULIS :
- 200 g caster sugar
- juice or zest of half a lemon
- 250 g ripe strawberries

PREPARATION

1.

Preheat your oven to th.6 (180 ° C). Reduce your "Small Butter" cookies to a fine powder using a food processor. Work the butter with a spatula so that it is soft and fold it into the cookie powder. Spread the preparation about 1 cm thick in a springform pan.

2.

Then wash the strawberries without soaking them, hull them and cut them into pieces then place them on your cheesecake base. Whisk the cottage cheese, sugar and eggs vigorously until you obtain a smooth and homogeneous cheesecake mixture. Pour this preparation over your pieces of strawberries. Bake your strawberry cheesecake for 40 min at th.6 (180 ° C).

3.

Prepare the coulis that will accompany your cheesecake by mixing together the strawberries, powdered sugar and lemon juice. At the end of cooking, let your cheesecake cool slightly in the refrigerator, then serve it with a generous amount of strawberry coulis.

5. Raspberry Cheesecake

INGREDIENTS

- 150 g dry cookies (of your choice)
- 80 g unsalted butter
- 75 g caster sugar
- 600 g of cream cheese
- 300 g of plain yogurt
- 3 tbsp. lemon juice
- 250 g of fresh raspberries

PREPARATION

1.

Melt the butter in the microwave and let it cool for a few minutes.

2.

Wash and dry the fresh raspberries thoroughly. Reserve them on absorbent paper.

3.

Reduce the dry cookies to a fine powder in a food processor or with a kitchen mortar.

4.

Mix the dry biscuit powder with the melted butter to obtain a homogeneous ball of shortbread dough.

5.

Line the bottom of a missed mold (to facilitate demolding) with the shortbread dough obtained and then press it down so that it is even over its entire surface. Keep cool while you prepare the cheesecake maker.

6.

In a bowl, using an electric mixer, whisk together the cream cheese, natural yogurt, powdered sugar, Agar-agar and lemon juice.

7.

Pour the cheesecake mixture on the bottom of the biscuit dough and set it aside in the refrigerator for at least 3 hours.

8.

When ready to serve, gently unmold your raspberry cheesecake without cooking and decorate it with fresh raspberries.

6. Pineapple cheesecake

INGREDIENTS

- 250 g of digestive biscuits
- 90 g melted butter
- 300 g of fresh cheese

- 1 C. heavy cream
- 20 g flour
- 160g caster sugar
- 1 medium whole egg
- 1 egg yolk
- juice of half a lemon
- 2 gelatin sheets

FOR THE GROUT:
- 1 fresh pineapple
- 1 C. tablespoons of brown sugar
- 1 C. lemon juice
- 1/2 tsp. vanilla powder

PREPARATION

1.

Soak the gelatin sheets in a bowl of cold water.

2.

Preheat the oven to 180 ° C.

3.

Mix the digestive biscuits in powder.

4.

Mix the cookie powder with the melted butter in a bowl until you get a sandy dough.

5.

Spread the sandy dough in the bottom of a springform pan covered with baking paper and placed on a baking sheet.

6.

Bake for 10 minutes.

7.

Leave to cool out of the oven.

8.

Wring out the gelatin sheets and melt them in a saucepan over low heat.

9.

Beat the whole egg and the egg yolk with the powdered sugar, the cream cheese, the juice of half a lemon and the crème fraîche in a bowl.

10.

Add the flour and melted gelatin and mix well.

11.

Pour the preparation on the biscuit base in the mold.

12.

Store in the freezer for a minimum of 3 hours.

13.

Meanwhile, prepare the coulis. Remove the rind, core and eyes from the pineapple. Cut it into thin slices.

14.

Cook the pineapple slices with the brown sugar, vanilla powder and lemon juice in a saucepan over high heat for 6 minutes.

15.

At the end of cooking, mix the mixture until you obtain a very thick coulis.

16.

Filter and reserve in the fridge.

17.

Three before serving, unmold the cheesecake and cover it with coulis.

18.

Decorate it with roasted or flambé pineapple slices (optional) and set aside until serving.

7. Avocado and Lemon Cheesecake

INGREDIENTS

- 160 g of chocolate cookies
- 50 g melted butter
- 4 limes
- 2 ripe avocados
- 400g Philadelphia® cheese
- 100 g of mascarpone
- 150g caster sugar
- 3 eggs
- 1 C. coffee

PREPARATION

1.

Take the zest of the 4 limes and grate it.

2.

Cut the limes in half and squeeze them to collect their juice.

3.

Pour the lemon juice into a saucepan.

4.

Add the grated zest, 80 g caster sugar and the cornstarch. Mix.

5.

Place the pan on low heat and let heat until thickened.

6.

Remove from the heat and let cool.

7.

Reduce the chocolate cookies to powder in a blender.

8.

Mix the cookie powder with the melted butter in a bowl until you get a sandy dough.

9.

Distribute the sandy dough in the bottom of a pastry ring covered with parchment paper. Tamp the surface well with your hands. Reserve in the fridge.

10.

Preheat the oven to 140 ° C.

11.

Take the flesh of the avocados and mix it in a blender until you obtain a smooth and homogeneous purée.

12.

Mix the avocado puree with the mascarpone in a salad bowl.

13.

Add the Philadelphia cheese and the rest of the powdered sugar. Whisk well.

14.

Add the eggs one at a time, then add half the thickened lime juice. Stir well.

15.

Pour the mixture over the sandy dough in the baking ring. Smooth the surface well with a spatula.

16.

Bake for 45 minutes.

17.

At the end of cooking, turn off the oven and let the cheesecake cool in the oven off for 1 hour.

18.

Then place it in the fridge for at least 12 hours before serving.

19.

When ready to serve, gently unmold the cheesecake and top it with the remaining thickened lemon juice.

20.

Decorate the cheesecake as you see fit and serve it chilled.

8. Knafeh Cheesecake

INGREDIENTS

FOR THE CAKE:
- 250 g of kadaif paste
- 50 g panko breadcrumbs
- 375 g fresh mozzarella
- 50 g very fine semolina
- 450 ml milk
- 250 g melted butter
- crushed pistachios

FOR THE SYRUP:
- 250 ml of water

- 250 g caster sugar
- 1 tbsp lemon juice
- 1 tbsp orange blossom water

PREPARATION

1.

Prepare the syrup.

2.

Bring the water with the sugar, lemon juice and orange blossom water to a boil in a saucepan, mixing well.

3.

Remove from the heat as soon as you obtain a syrup.

4.

Book.

5.

Prepare the cake:

6.

Mix the kadaif paste in a blender until you get a fine powder.

7.

Pour it into a bowl, add the melted butter and 125 g of the lukewarm syrup, mixing well.

8.

Press the mixture into the bottom of a baking ring lined with parchment paper.

9.

Reserve in the fridge.

10.

Preheat the oven to 200 ° C.

11.

Heat the milk in a saucepan.

12.

Add the semolina in rain and mix with a whisk until the preparation thickens.

13.

Beat the mascarpone in a salad bowl.

14.

Add the milk-semolina mixture, beating well.

15.

Pour everything over the crusty base in the mold.

16.

Bake for 45 minutes.

17.

Take out of the oven and let stand for 15 minutes.

18.

Turn out onto a serving platter

19.

Soak with 50 ml of syrup.

20.

Decorate with the crushed pistachios.

21.

Serve hot with the rest of the syrup.

9. Pistachio Cheesecake

INGREDIENTS

FOR THE SANDY BISCUIT:

- 250 g of Breton shortbread
- 125 g butter
- 3 tbsp. pistachio paste

FOR THE CHEESECAKE MACHINE:

- 600 g of plain Philadelphia cheese (or Saint-Môret)
- 150 g icing sugar
- 3 eggs
- 2 egg yolks
- 20 cl of fresh cream
- 3 tbsp. tablespoon flour

- 2 tbsp. lemon juice
- 2 tbsp. vanilla extract
- a few crushed pistachios for decoration

PREPARATION

1.

Make the sanded base:

2.

Crush the Breton shortbread then mix them with the melted butter and the pistachio paste, until you obtain a sandy mixture.

3.

Tamp the mixture at the bottom of a pastry ring placed on a baking sheet covered with baking paper, pressing well.

4.

Reserve in the fridge.

5.

Make the cheesecake maker:

6.

Preheat the oven to 170 ° C.

7.

Whip the philadelphia using a mixer.

8.

Incorporate the sugar while continuing to whisk then the whole eggs and the egg yolks, the sour cream and the flour. Whisk vigorously but quickly until a homogeneous mixture is obtained.

9.

Pour the device into the circle, smoothing the surface well.

10.

Bake for 30 minutes then continue cooking at 150 ° C for 30 minutes.

11.

When it comes out of the oven, the cheesecake should be foamy in the center.

12.

Let the cheesecake cool to room temperature then put it in the fridge for several hours.

13.

Turn out the cheesecake before serving.

14.

Decorate the surface with a few crushed pistachios.

15.

Enjoy well chilled.

10. Dukan Cheesecake

INGREDIENTS

- 400 gr of cottage cheese 0% fat
- 6 small fresh squares 0% fat
- 3 eggs
- 1 untreated lemon
- 1.5 tbsp. teaspoon liquid sweetener
- 1/2 tsp. level coffee of vanilla beans

- 1 C. teaspoon agar-agar

PREPARATION

1.

Preheat the oven to th.6 (180 ° C),

2.

Drain the cottage cheese, placing it for several hours in a colander, the bottom of which is covered with absorbent paper.

3.

Mash the fresh squares in a bowl, add the cottage cheese, eggs, sweetener and vanilla beans. Mix to obtain a homogeneous preparation then add the lemon zest and the agar-agar.

4.

Leave to stand for 15 min then pour into a silicone mold, smooth the top of the cheesecake with a spatula then bake for 15 min.

5.

Then lower the oven to th. 3 (100 ° C) for 40 to 50 minutes. Check the doneness by appreciating the firmness of the cake.

6.

When the cheesecake has the right consistency, leave it in the oven off, with the oven door ajar, until it cools.

7.

Let stand at least 6 to 8 hours in the fridge before tasting.

11. Redberry Cheesecake

INGREDIENTS

- 250 g of mascarpone
- 250 g ricotta
- 1 packet of shortbread cookies
- 200 g blueberries
- 200 g raspberries
- 180 g icing sugar
- 150g butter

PREPARATION

1.

Gently crush the cookies. Melt the butter and mix together in a bowl. Line a springform pan with the mixture, and set aside at least 30 minutes in the refrigerator to harden the dough.

2.

While your dough is cool, in a deep plate, mix the ricotta and mascarpone with 130 grams of icing sugar. Beat vigorously.

3.

Remove your dough from the fridge and spread your ricotta-mascarpone mixture over the dough.

4.

Put everything back in the fridge for at least 2 hours.

5.

Clean the blueberries and raspberries. Reserve 1/3 of the fruit, pour the rest into a saucepan.

6.

Add the remaining icing sugar and heat over low heat to make a compote.

7.

When the compote is ready, let cool before spreading it on the cheesecake. Finish by sprinkling with raspberries and whole blueberries.

12. Tuna Cheesecake

INGREDIENTS

- 1 package of salted crackers
- 100 g butter
- 300 g of cream cheese
- 1 can tuna in brine, drained
- 2 eggs
- 2 tbsp. chopped parsley
- the juice of a lemon
- salt pepper

PREPARATION

1.

Preheat the oven to 200 ° C.

2.

Crumble the crackers.

3.

Mix them with the melted butter until you get a sandy dough.

4.

Line with the bottom of a loaf pan covered with parchment paper.

5.

Reserve aside.

6.

Crumble the tuna.

7.

Mix it with the cream cheese, eggs and lemon juice.

8.

Add the parsley, salt and pepper then mix well.

9.

Pour over the biscuit base in the mold.

10.

Bake for 15 minutes.

11.

Let cool at room temperature.

12.

Unmould and keep in the fridge until serving.

13. Smoked Salmon Cheesecake

INGREDIENTS

- 8 Fresh Square (200 g)
- 4 slices of smoked salmon
- 110 g of salted crackers
- 70 g butter
- 2 eggs
- 1 bunch of chives
- 2 tbsp. 20% cottage cheese
- juice of a lemon
- salt, freshly ground pepper

PREPARATION

1.

Preheat the oven th.5 (150 ° C).

2.

Melt the butter in a saucepan.

3.

Crush the crackers in a bowl and mix them with the melted butter. Spread this mixture on the bottom of a springform pan (with removable bottom, if possible).

4.

Chop the chives. Reserve a few sprigs for decoration.

5.

Beat the eggs in a bowl. Add the Carré Frais, the fromage blanc, 2 slices of salmon cut into small pieces, the chives and the lemon juice. Add salt and pepper. Mix everything well.

6.

Spread the preparation on the crackers.

7.

Bake and cook for 40 min. Let the cheesecake cool to room temperature then set aside for at least 4 hours in the refrigerator.

8.

When ready to serve, turn out the cheesecake and decorate the surface with the rest of the smoked salmon cut into strips and the reserved chives.

14. Peach Cheesecake

INGREDIENTS

- 110 g of cookies
- 2 eggs
- 300 g of cream cheese
- 50 g of brown sugar
- 300 g of cottage cheese
- 1 C. liquid vanilla
- 2 tbsp. tablespoon of cane sugar
- 3 ripe peaches
- 30 cl of peach syrup

PREPARATION

1.

Preheat the oven to 210 ° C.

2.

Crumble the cookies.

3.

Line the bottom of a baking pan lined with parchment paper, packing well.

4.

Reserve in the fridge.

5.

In a salad bowl, mix the cheeses and the brown sugar.

6.

Add cane sugar and liquid vanilla then stir well.

7.

Add the eggs and mix well until a smooth mixture is obtained.

8.

Pour the dough over the cookies in the pan.

9.

Bake for 40 minutes.

10.

Let cool out of the oven then unmold the cheesecake.

11.

Clean, pit and cut the peaches into thin slices.

12.

Place them on the cheesecake.

13.

Store the cake in the refrigerator for at least 8 hours.

14.

Serve the cheesecake topped with the peach syrup.

15. Cheesecake with salted butter caramel sauce

INGREDIENTS

FOR THE BISCUITÉE BASE:
- 200 g of cookies
- 50 g sugar
- 70 g butter

FOR THE APPLIANCE:
- 600g plain butter
- 100 g sugar
- 3 eggs
- 1 sachet of vanilla sugar

FOR THE SALTED BUTTER CARAMEL:
- 100 g sugar

- 125 ml of liquid cream
- 30 g salted butter
- 1 C. tablespoon of water

PREPARATION

1.

Prepare the cheesecake:

2.

Reduce the cookies to powder.

3.

Melt the butter.

4.

Mix the cookies, sugar and melted butter until you get a sandy dough.

5.

Line with the bottom of a loaf pan covered with parchment paper.

6.

Reserve in the fridge.

7.

Preheat the oven to 150 ° C.

8.

In a bowl, mix the butter with the sugar.

9.

Add the eggs one at a time and mix until the mixture is smooth and smooth. Pour the preparation on the biscuit base in the mold.

10.

Sprinkle the cheesecake with the bag of vanilla sugar.

11.

Bake for 50 minutes.

12.

Let the cheesecake cool in the oven off.

13.

Keep refrigerated for at least 12 hours.

14.

Prepare the salted butter caramel:

15.

Melt without mixing the sugar with the water in a saucepan until the caramel is colored.

16.

Add the butter cut into pieces then the liquid cream, stirring lightly.

17.

Let heat until the caramel thickens.

18.

Remove from the heat and let cool.

19.

When ready to serve, turn out the cheesecake and serve it topped with salted butter caramel sauce.

16.   Chocolate Cheesecake

INGREDIENTS

FOR THE DOUGH BASE:
- 150 g of cookies (Pepito type)
- 90 g semi-salted butter

FOR THE CHOCOLATE CHEESECAKE :
- 4 whole eggs
- 90 g caster sugar
- 200 g dark chocolate
- 300 g plain cream cheese (Philadelphia type)
- 100 g of plain faisselle
- 100 g of liquid cream.

PREPARATION

1.

Preheat your oven to th.4 / 5 (145 ° C).

2.

Melt the butter in the microwave or in a saucepan (be careful not to overcook it).

3.

In a food processor, mix the cookies into a fine powder. Then add the melted butter to obtain a pastry base for your chocolate cheesecake.

4.

In a pastry ring covered with parchment paper (or aluminum foil), roll out your pastry base then press it down so that it is homogeneous over its entire surface.

5.

Break the chocolate into pieces and melt it in a double boiler. Mix it so that it is homogeneous and set aside for a few minutes to let it cool.

6.

Carefully drain the faisselle.

7.

Separate the egg whites from the yolks. Whip the egg whites until stiff and set them aside.

8.

In a bowl, whisk together the cream cheese, the drained faisselle, the liquid cream and the sugar. Then add the egg yolks and melted chocolate. Mix well.

9.

Then fold in the snowy egg whites delicately using a spatula.

10.

Pour your Easy Chocolate Cheesecake Maker over your pastry base.

11.

Place your pastry ring containing the cheesecake in a double boiler then bake for 40 minutes at th.4 / 5 (145 ° C).

12.

At the end of cooking, reserve your easy chocolate cheesecake in the refrigerator for 3 hours before unmolding it.

17. White Chocolate Cheesecake

INGREDIENTS

- 100 g unsalted butter
- 1 egg white
- 25g caster sugar
- 275 g white chocolate

- 225 g plain cream cheese (preferably half-salt)
- 150 g of plain yogurt
- 5 cl of orange juice (approximately 1 special orange juice)
- 250 g of tea biscuits.

PREPARATION

1.

Melt the butter in the microwave and let it cool slightly.

2.

In your food processor, reduce the tea cookies to a fine powder. Add the melted butter and mix until you obtain a smooth and homogeneous dough base.

3.

Spread your dough base in a pie mold (or a missed mold to facilitate demolding) and keep it cool for 30 minutes.

4.

Melt the white chocolate in a double boiler, mix to obtain a homogeneous chocolate sauce and let it cool for a few minutes.

5.

In a salad bowl, whisk together the cream cheese, plain yogurt, sugar, orange juice and melted white chocolate.

6.

Whip the egg white until stiff then fold it gently into the previous preparation using a spatula.

7.

Pour your white chocolate cheesecake machine on your pastry base.

8.

Reserve your cheesecake in the refrigerator for 1 night before delicately unmolding it.

9.

Serve your white chocolate cheese-cake cool.

18. Lime and Kiwi Cheesecake

INGREDIENTS

- 100 g of cookies of your choice (shortbread, small butters ...)
- 40 g melted butter
- 15 centiliters of liquid cream
- 300 g of fresh cheese like Philadelphia or Saint-Môret
- 50 g of sugar + or - if you have a sweet tooth
- 2 limes, preferably organic
- 4 kiwis

PREPARATION

1.

Mix your cookies more or less finely according to your preference. Mix them in a bowl with the melted butter. Place your pastry circles on a baking sheet covered with baking paper or directly in your serving plates. Distribute the cookie crumbs in the bottom of your circles, packing them well. Store in a cool place while you prepare the rest of the recipe.

2.

Peel and blend a kiwi.

3.

In a salad bowl, with a whisk or with an electric mixer, use the cream cheese with the zest of the 2 limes and the juice of one and the sugar. Adjust the amount of sugar to your liking if you like sweet desserts.

4.

In another bowl, whip the liquid cream into whipped cream. Gently fold the whipped cream into your cream cheese in several batches.

5.

Distribute half of this preparation on the biscuit bases while going up on the edges so as to form a hole to pour in a little mixed kiwi. Gently drop the rest of your preparation in your circles and smooth the surface. Cover with cling film and store in the refrigerator for 24 hours.

6.

On the day of tasting, gently unmold your cheesecakes using a pusher. Peel and thinly slice 2 or 3 kiwis and arrange them on top of your cheesecakes. Optionally add a few lime zest, serve and enjoy.

19. Coffee Cheesecake

INGREDIENTS

FOR THE CAKE:
- 200 g of digestive biscuits
- 40 g of soft butter
- 20 g unsweetened bitter cocoa
- 700 g of cream cheese
- 6 g of soluble coffee dissolved in half a cup of hot water
- 4 eggs
- 175 g sugar

FOR THE SAUCE:
- 50 g dark chocolate
- 35 g of water
- caramel sauce

PREPARATION

1.

Preheat the oven to 150 ° C.

2.

Crumble the digestive biscuits.

3.

Mix them in a bowl with the soft butter and cocoa powder until you get a sandy mixture.

4.

Spread the preparation in the bottom of a baking tin, packing well.

5.

Reserve in the refrigerator.

6.

In a salad bowl, mix together the cream cheese, cottage cheese and sugar.

7.

Add the whole eggs one by one, then the cold coffee, mixing well.

8.

Pour the appliance onto the biscuit base of the mold.

9.

Bake for 40 minutes.

10.

Leave to cool to room temperature after removing from the oven.

11.

Then store in the refrigerator for 12 hours.

12.

After resting time, unmold and set aside in the fridge until serving.

13.

Prepare the sauce by melting the dark chocolate with the whiskey and water in a saucepan over a double boiler until you obtain a smooth sauce.

14.

Reserve at room temperature until serving.

15.

Serve the cheesecake cold topped with chocolate sauce and caramel sauce.

20. Vanilla and Cacao Cheesecake

INGREDIENTS

FOR THE VANILLA TOPPING:
- 700 g of white cheese 0%
- 3 tbsp. tablespoon of agave syrup (or 80 g of sugar)
- 4 eggs
- 2 tbsp. tablespoons of cornstarch (or flour)
- 1 C. 1 teaspoon of natural vanilla extract

FOR THE CHOCOLATE COOKIE CRUST:
- 150 g of Breton palet type cookies
- 80 g of 70% cocoa chocolate
- 30g butter

PREPARATION

1.

Preheat the oven to th. 5 (150 ° C).

2.

Preparation of the chocolate biscuit crust:

3.

Mix the cookies in a blender and add the butter and melted chocolate.

4.

Then line the bottom of the mold with baking paper and spread the preparation using the back of a tablespoon at the start and the bottom of a glass to tamp the preparation then. This will also serve to homogenize the thickness. Keep refrigerated while you prepare the filling.

5.

Preparation of the light and vanilla filling:

6.

Whisk the eggs and the agave syrup (or the sugar), add the cornstarch sifted in rain, the vanilla and finally the cottage cheese.

7.

Mix everything by hand or in a food processor to obtain a homogeneous mixture. Mix one last time.

8.

Distribute this filling over the biscuit crust and bake for about 45 min.

9.

Let cool and set aside for several hours in the fridge.

10.

Turn out, decorate with cocoa and serve.

21.   Lime Cheesecake

INGREDIENTS

- 225 g cream cheese
- 50 g heavy cream
- 1 lime (lime)
- 125 g of dry biscuits
- 63 g melted butter
- 1 egg
- 65g caster sugar

PREPARATION

1.

Preheat your oven to 180 ° C.

2.

In a bowl, melt the butter in the microwave.

3.

Crumble the cookies then add them to the butter.

4.

Mix everything.

5.

Line with the bottom of a loaf pan covered with parchment paper.

6.

Place in the refrigerator for 30 minutes.

7.

In a bowl, break your egg and beat it into an omelet.

8.

Grate your lemon then on a kitchen board, slice it in 2.

9.

Squeeze it and collect the juice in a bowl.

10.

In another bowl, mix the crème fraîche and fromage frais.

11.

Add the egg, sugar, lemon juice and lemon zest to the previous mixture.

12.

Mix again.

13.

Pour the resulting cream into the mold.

14.

Bake for 30 minutes.

15.

Turn off the oven and let the cheesecake warm for another 1/2 hour.

16.

Return to the refrigerator for at least 6 hours.

17.

Unmould and cut into equal parts.

18.

Serve the small cheesecakes very fresh decorated with a thin slice of lime.

22. Caramel and Speculoos Cheesecake

INGREDIENTS

FOR THE DOUGH:
- 175 g of speculoos
- 50 g melted butter

FOR THE CARAMEL:
- 100 g of brown sugar

- 100 g icing sugar
- 60 g butter
- 5 c. tablespoon of water
- 2 tbsp. of milk

FOR THE CHEESE MIX:
- 500 g of mascarpone
- 250 g ricotta
- 150 g sugar
- 4 eggs
- the juice of 2 lemons
- 2 tbsp. vanilla extract

PREPARATION

1.

Preheat the oven th.6 (180 ° C).

2.

Prepare the dough:

3.

Melt the butter. Crush the cookies to obtain a coarse crumb. Mix.

4.

Line a springform pan with parchment paper. Distribute the dough in the bottom of the mold and on the sides of it, packing well. Bake for 8 to 15 minutes.

5.

Prepare the cream:

6.

Beat the ricotta with an electric whisk to make it creamier. Add the sugar and the mascarpone, beat.

7.

Add the lemon juice and vanilla and beat again. Then add the eggs one by one to the preparation.

8.

Mix well.

9.

Bake for 1 hour at 5/6 (160 ° C), let cool then leave in the fridge for at least 3 hours.

10.

Prepare the caramel:

11.

In a saucepan, put the butter and brown sugar. (Do not stop stirring so as not to let the preparation boil). Once the butter has melted, add the milk, still stirring, then add the water little by little. Once the brown sugar is brown, remove from the heat and add the icing sugar while stirring constantly. Let cool.

12.

Cover the cheesecake with the caramel and leave in the fridge until dessert.

13.

Serve and enjoy.

23. Cheesecake with ricotta and fresh lemon cheese

INGREDIENTS

- 100 g of sweet cookies
- 300 g light ricotta
- 200 g light cream cheese
- 8 cl of lemon juice
- grated lemon zest
- 75g light rapeseed margarine
- 125 g caster sugar
- 2 eggs

PREPARATION

1.

Preheat your oven to 160 ° C (th.5-6).

2.

Put the equivalent of 2 tbsp. grated lemon zest in a suitable container then set aside.

3.

Take a mold.

4.

Grease it then line it with baking paper.

5.

Put the cookies in a suitable mortar and crush them.

6.

Then collect these crushed cookies and put them in a deep plate.

7.

Add the margarine and mix well.

8.

Line the bottom of the mold with this mixture, pressing with the bottom of a glass.

9.

Place this mold in a refrigerator for 30 min.

10.

In a salad bowl, put the ricotta.

11.

Add the cream cheese, lemon juice and 3 tbsp. grated lemon zest.

12.

With an electric mixer, mix everything well to obtain a homogeneous consistency.

13.

Crack a whole egg on top of this bowl.

14.

Break another egg into 2 separate containers, separating the white from the yolk.

15.

Add the egg white to the bowl mixture.

16.

Mix everything thoroughly.

17.

Pour this preparation finally obtained, in your mold then sprinkle the surface with the rest of lemon zest.

18.

Bake for 45 min.

19.

Make sure you don't let the center take completely.

20.

At the end of the cooking time, remove the mold from the oven and let this cake cool.

21.

Then put it in the refrigerator for 5 hours.

22.

Remove it from the fridge.

24.   White Cheese and Speculoos Cheesecake

INGREDIENTS

- 175 g of crumbled speculoos (or small butter)
- 10 Cracotte
- 60 g light butter, melted
- 700 g of cottage cheese 0% fat
- 3 tbsp. liquid sweetener

- 1 C. tablespoon flour
- 1 egg
- 20 cl of liquid cream 3% fat

PREPARATION

1.

Preheat the oven to 180 ° C.

2.

Preferably take a silicone mold of small diameter but with high edges so that the cheesecake can have a nice thickness. If you don't have a silicone mold, use baking paper to make it easier to unmold your cheesecake.

3.

Crumble the biscuits and cracottes: you can mix them or put them in a freezer bag and reduce them to crumbs with a glass or a tin can for example.

4.

Once the biscuits and cracottes mixture is crumbled, add the melted butter and mix to obtain a homogeneous preparation. Line the bottom of the mold with this mixture: make sure to flatten it well with the back of a tablespoon. The mixture should be evenly distributed.

5.

Put the mold in the refrigerator.

6.

Then mix in a salad bowl the fromage blanc, the cream, the sweetener, the flour, then the egg and pour everything into the mold over the biscuit-cracotte mixture.

7.

Bake for about 50 minutes. The cheesecake must be firm.

8.

Let cool then unmold.

25. Mango Cheesecake

INGREDIENTS

- 350 g of digestive biscuits
- 150 g melted butter
- 6 cans of mangoes in syrup
- 500 g of cottage cheese
- 30 cl of heavy cream
- 250 g caster sugar
- 2 eggs
- 9 gelatin sheets

PREPARATION

1.

Reduce the digestive biscuits to powder using a blender.

2.

Mix the crushed cookies with the melted butter in a bowl, until you get a very sandy mixture.

3.

Spread the preparation in a pastry ring placed on a flat support, packing it well with your fingers.

4.

Reserve in the refrigerator the time to prepare the appliance.

5.

Soften 8 gelatin sheets in a bowl of cold water.

6.

Separate the egg whites from the yolks.

7.

Drain the mangoes, reserving half of the pieces aside, for the coulis, plus a glass of juice for the appliance.

8.

Mash the mangoes with a blender, then add the fromage blanc, crème fraîche, powdered sugar and egg yolks.

9.

Heat the mango syrup in a saucepan and melt the squeezed gelatin in it. Mix it with the curd cheese mixture.

10.

Beat the egg whites until stiff and incorporate them into the preparation.

11.

Mix well then pour the mixture onto the biscuit base in the pastry ring, smoothing the surface with a spatula.

12.

Harden in the refrigerator for at least 4 hours.

13.

Soften the remaining gelatin sheet in a bowl of cold water.

14.

Mix the reserved mango pieces with a little water, using a blender, until you obtain a very smooth and homogeneous fruit coulis.

15.

Pour the coulis into a saucepan over low heat and heat it until it boils.

16.

When it comes to the boil, remove the pan from the heat and pour the squeezed gelatin into the coulis. Stir well.

17.

Pour the mango coulis over the cheesecake.

18.

Put it back in the fridge for at least 1 hour before tasting.

19.

Unmold just before serving.

20.

Enjoy well chilled.

26. BlueBerry Cheesecake

INGREDIENTS

- 500 g of fresh blueberries
- 150 g of cookies
- 125 g applesauce
- 4 eggs
- 500 g of mascarpone
- 250 g ricotta
- 150 g sugar
- 2 tbsp. tablespoon flour
- 1 sachet of vanilla sugar
- 2 gelatin sheets

PREPARATION

1.

Preheat the oven to 180 ° C.

2.

Crumble the cookies.

3.

Mix them with the applesauce in a bowl until you get a sandy dough.

4.

Line the mixture in the bottom of a loaf pan lined with parchment paper.

5.

Reserve in the fridge.

6.

Beat the mascarpone and the ricotta in a bowl.

7.

Add the flour, sugar, vanilla sugar and eggs then mix well.

8.

Pour the mixture into the mold, smoothing the surface well.

9.

Bake the cheesecake for 40 minutes.

10.

Let the cheesecake cool in the oven off.

11.

Then put it in the fridge for at least 3 hours.

12.

Soften the gelatin sheets in a bowl of cold water.

13.

Clean and pat dry the blueberries.

14.

Mix 350 g of blueberries in a blender until you obtain a coulis.

15.

Pass the coulis through a Chinese to remove the grains.

16.

Heat the coulis in a saucepan over low heat.

17.

Off the heat, add the gelatin and mix well.

18.

Crush the rest of the fresh blueberries using a pestle.

19.

Add them to the pot and stir.

20.

Cover the cold cheesecake with the coulis, smoothing well.

21.

Place in the fridge for another 3 hours.

22.

Turn out to serve.

23.

Enjoy well chilled.

27. Paleo Coco Cheesecake

INGREDIENTS

FOR THE BOTTOM:
- 125 g grated coconut
- 1 egg
- 25 g of coconut powder
- 2 tbsp. chopped walnuts
- 1 C. grated lemon zest
- 7 cl of coconut oil
- 2 tbsp. of honey

FOR GARNISH :
- 30 cl of coconut cream

- 250 g of ground hazelnuts
- 5 eggs
- 3 tbsp. of honey
- 3 tbsp. butter, melted
- 3 tbsp. lemon juice
- 2 tbsp. grated lemon zest
- 1 C. vanilla extract
- 1 pinch of salt

PREPARATION

1.

Prepare the bottom:

2.

Mix all the ingredients until you get a homogeneous mixture.

3.

Spread the mixture in the bottom of a removable mold covered with baking paper.

4.

Reserve aside.

5.

Prepare the filling:

6.

Crate and beat the eggs in a bowl.

7.

Add the coconut cream, melted butter, lemon juice and vanilla extract and mix well.

8.

Incorporate the ground hazelnuts, lemon zest and salt then stir until you obtain a homogeneous mixture.

9.

Pour the mixture over the bottom into the mold. Level the surface with a spatula.

10.

Store the cheesecake in the fridge for 8 hours.

11.

Carefully unmold and cut into equal parts.

12.

Serve chilled with a homemade fruit coulis.

28. Apple Cheesecake

INGREDIENTS

- 3 apples
- lemon juice
- 250 g of "small brown" cookies
- 125 g butter
- 500 g of cottage cheese
- 150 g sugar
- 2 tbsp. tablespoon flour
- 3 eggs
- 25 cl of fresh cream
- Sesame seeds

PREPARATION

1.

Preheat the oven th.6 (180 ° C).

2.

Line a round mold with removable bottom with parchment paper.

3.

Peel and finely slice 2 apples.

4.

Crumble the cookies finely.

5.

Melt the butter.

6.

Combine crumbled cookies and melted butter until a dough forms. Line the bottom of the mold with it, packing well.

7.

Then arrange on top of the apple slices and place in the fridge.

8.

Whisk in the cottage cheese until smooth. Add the sugar, flour and then the eggs one by one, whisking constantly. Finish with the crème fraîche.

9.

Pour the preparation into the mold and put in the oven and cook for 55 min.

10.

In the meantime, wash the remaining apple and slice it into very thin slices. Sprinkle with lemon juice and place in the fridge in cling film.

11.

Take the cheese cake out of the oven, let it cool before putting it in the fridge.

12.

Turn out the cake in a dish, cover it with apple slices and sprinkle with sesame seeds.

13.

Serve chilled.

29. Orange Cheesecake

INGREDIENTS

FOR THE DOUGH:
- 110 g flour
- 50 g sugar
- 2 young eggs
- 140 g of soft butter (110g + 30g)
- 1 pinch of salt

FOR GARNISH:
- 800 g of white cheese
- 200 g sugar
- 100 g of fresh flour
- 6 eggs
- 2 untreated oranges

- cream
- some candied orange zest
- a few grains of sugar
- 2 sprigs of mint

PREPARATION

1.

Preheat the oven th. 6 (180°C).

2.

Drain the fromage blanc in a strainer lined with muslin for 4 hours. Butter a mold with removable edge and line the bottom with buttered parchment paper. Prepare the dough. Place the flour, sugar, egg yolks, butter and salt in the bowl of a food processor. Mix until the dough forms a ball and spread it in the bottom of the mold by pressing with your fingertips. Bake for 15 min.

3.

Meanwhile, put the drained cottage cheese, sugar, flour, grated zest from the 2 oranges, eggs and cream in the bowl of the food processor and mix until the preparation is smooth. Pour it into the mold, smooth it with a spatula and continue cooking for 15 minutes. Then lower the oven th.4 (120°C) and bake for 1 hour 15 minutes.

4.

Let the cake cool completely before unmolding it, decorate it with candied orange zest, raw peeled quarters taken from the 2 oranges and sprigs of mint then sprinkle the outline with sugar grains. Serve chilled.

30. Cacao Cheesecake

INGREDIENTS

FOR THE BASE:
- 150 g of sweet cookies
- 2 tbsp. cocoa powder
- 6 c. butter, melted

FOR THE APPLIANCE:
- 300 g of cottage cheese
- 70 g sugar
- 50 g of almond powder
- 20g cocoa powder

- 2 eggs
- 1 teaspoon of vanilla flavoring
- Cocoa Powder
- Chocolate chips

PREPARATION

1.

Prepare the biscuit base:

2.

Crumble the cookies into powder.

3.

Mix them with the cocoa and butter until you get a biscuit dough.

4.

Line with the bottom of a removable mold placed on a baking sheet covered with parchment paper.

5.

Prepare the device:

6.

Preheat the oven to 180 ° C.

7.

Separate the egg whites from the yolks.

8.

Mix the yolks with the sugar.

9.

Add the cocoa, almond powder and vanilla then the fromage blanc, mixing well.

10.

Whip the egg whites until stiff and gently incorporate them into the preparation.

11.

Pour the appliance onto the biscuit base in the mold.

12.

Bake for 1 hour.

13.

Let the cheesecake cool for 1 hour in the oven off.

14.

Keep refrigerated until serving.

15.

Turn out to serve.

16.

Sprinkle with cocoa powder and chocolate shavings.

17.

Enjoy well chilled.

31. Apricot juice

INGREDIENTS

- 6 apricots
- 1 plain yogurt with 0% fat
- 200 g of cottage cheese with 0% fat
- 2 eggs and 1 white
- 30 g of cornstarch
- a little margarine

PREPARATION

1.

Preheat the oven to 150 ° C (th.5).

2.

Butter a cake pan.

3.

Cut the apricots in half and remove the pit. Then cut them into quarters.

4.

In a saucepan, mix the cornstarch with the yogurt over medium heat. Mix until thickened.

5.

Add the cottage cheese and mix vigorously.

6.

Off the heat, stir in the egg yolks, one at a time.

7.

In a salad bowl, beat the egg whites until stiff, then without stopping beating, very delicately incorporate the dairy preparation.

8.

Pour the preparation into a greased mold.

9.

Smooth the surface and place the apricot quarters on it.

10.

Bake and cook for about 1 hour.

11.

Turn out the cheesecake and let it cool before serving.

32. Tomato Cheesecake

INGREDIENTS

- 100 g of salted crackers
- 1 can of Mutti Basil Polpa
- 200 g of fresh goat cheese
- 150 g ricotta
- 100 g butter
- 100 g whipping cream
- 2 g of agar-agar

PREPARATION

1.

Grind the crackers and mix them with the butter.

2.

Tamp this mixture into the bottom of a pop-up mold and set aside in the refrigerator.

3.

Whip the fresh goat cheese, the ricotta and the heavy cream until a smooth mixture is obtained.

4.

Pour this preparation over the cracker base.

5.

In a saucepan, bring the Polpa and agar-agar to a boil. Let cool and pour over the cheese cream. Leave to set in the refrigerator.

6.

Serve chilled sprinkled with basil leaves.

33. Mango and Speculoos Cheesecake

INGREDIENTS

- 70g melted butter
- 200g of speculoos
- 6 cl of liquid cream
- 4 eggs
- 2 egg yolks
- 40g flour
- 250g sugar
- 850g cream cheese
- A knob of butter
- 100g of sugar
- 2 mangoes

PREPARATION

1.

Prepare the base of the cheesecake by roughly mixing the speculoos. Then add the melted butter and mix everything. Distribute in the bottom of your removable mold. Bake for 7 minutes at 180 ° C.

2.

Let cool and during this time beat the cream cheese with the sugar. Add the crème fraîche, then the eggs, egg yolks, flour and vanilla. Mix well to obtain a homogeneous paste. Pour the preparation on the biscuit dough and bake again for 1 hour at 180 ° C.

3.

For the mangoes, peel them and cut them into pieces. Brown them in the pan with the butter and sugar. Serve the cheesecake with the caramelized mangoes on top.

ENJOY .

Printed in Great Britain
by Amazon